Congregation for the
Doctrine of the Faith

INSTRUCTION ON SOME ASPECTS OF THE USE OF THE INSTRUMENTS OF SOCIAL COMMUNICATION IN PROMOTING THE DOCTRINE OF THE FAITH

St. Paul Books & Media

ISBN 0-8198-3666-4

Vatican Translation

Printed and published in the U.S.A. by St. Paul Books & Media, 50 St. Paul's Avenue, Boston, MA 02130

St. Paul Books & Media is the publishing house of the Daughters of St. Paul, an international congregation of women religious serving the Church with the communications media.

1 2 3 4 5 6 7 8 9   99 98 97 96 95 94 93 92

Contents

Introduction

The Second Vatican Council reminds us that among the principal duties of bishops "the preaching of the Gospel occupies an eminent place" *(Lumen Gentium,* 25). This is in keeping with the mission given by the Lord to teach all nations and to preach the Gospel to every creature (cf. Mt. 28:19).

The social communications media surely have to be counted among the most effective instruments available today for spreading the message of the Gospel. Not only does the church claim the right to use them (cf. Canon 747); she also encourages bishops to take advantage of them in fulfilling their mission (cf. Canon 822.1).

The decree of the Second Vatican Council *Inter Mirifica* and the Pontifical Council for Social Communications' pastoral instructions *Communio et Progressio* and *Aetatis Novae* have already given full treatment to the importance of the social communications media and their place in light of the church's mission to evangelize. Mention likewise should be made of the "Guide to the Training of Future Priests Concerning the Instruments of Social Communication" issued by the Congregation for Catholic Education.

The new Code of Canon Law also deals with the instruments of social communication (Canons 822-832) and entrusts their care and supervision to the bishops. Religious superiors, especially major superiors, also have specific responsibilities in this regard by virtue of their disciplinary authority.

The difficulties encountered for various reasons by those who are called to the care and supervision of the media are well known. Still, erroneous ideas are becoming ever more widespread due to the social communications media in general and the publication of books in particular. With the publication of its *Instruction on the Ecclesial Vocation of the Theologian* on May 24, 1990, the Congregation for the Doctrine of the Faith offered from the doctrinal perspective an outline of the responsibilities bishops have with regard to the authentic magisterium. In accordance with its mission to promote and defend the church's teaching on faith and morals, this same congregation has judged it good to issue the present instruction, which has been prepared in agreement with the Congregation for Institutes of Consecrated Life and Societies of Apostolic Life and after due consultation with the Pontifical Council for Social Communications.

The instruction sets forth the pertinent legislation of the church in an organic fashion. Its aim is to give encouragement and help to the bishops in the fulfillment of their obligations (cf. Canon 34) by calling to mind the norms of canon law, explaining their various provisions, and defining and making explicit the processes by which they are implemented.

The norms of canon law guarantee the freedom of all: whether it be the individual Christian faithful who have a right to receive the Gospel message in all its integrity and purity or those engaged in pastoral work, theologians and all Catholics engaged in journalism who have the right to communicate their thought while maintaining the integrity of the faith and the church's teaching on morals and due respect for the bishops. By the same token, civil laws regarding the dissemination of information should protect and foster the right of all who use the social communications media to a truthful presentation of the facts. They likewise assure journalists in general of the right to communicate their thought within the limits of a professional code of ethics which also has concern for the way in which religious topics are handled.

The Congregation for the Doctrine of the Faith is aware of the difficult conditions under which theologians, those engaged in pastoral work, Catholic journalists and journalists in general must labor in the fulfillment of their tasks. Thus it feels it right here to express a particular word of esteem and appreciation to them for the contribution they make with their efforts in this field.

I.

Bishops' Responsibilities in General

1. The Responsibility of Instructing the Faithful

1. Bishops, inasmuch as they are authentic teachers of the faith (cf. Canons 375 and 753), must take care to instruct the faithful concerning the right and duty they have to:

a) "Work so that the divine message of salvation may increasingly reach the whole of humankind in every age and in every land" (Canon 211).

b) Make known their needs, especially spiritual ones, and their desires to the pastors of the church (cf. Canon 212.2).

c) Manifest to the pastors their opinion on matters which pertain to the good of the church (cf. Canon 212.3).

d) Make their own opinion as to what pertains to the good of the church known to others of the Christian faithful "with due regard for the integrity of faith and morals and reverence toward their pastors and with consideration for the common good and the dignity of persons" (Canon 212.3).

2. The faithful are also to be instructed in their duty to:

a) "Maintain always, even in their own patterns of activity, communion with the church" (Canon 209.1; cf. Canon 205).

b) "Follow by Christian obedience what the sacred pastors, as representatives of Christ, declare as teachers of the faith or determine as leaders of the church" (Canon 212.1).

c) Observe due respect for the magisterium of the church if they are engaged in the sacred disciplines even while they enjoy a lawful freedom of inquiry and of prudently expressing their opinions on matters in which they have expertise (cf. Canon 218).

d) Cooperate so that the use of the instruments of social communication is animated with a human and Christian spirit (cf. Canon 822.2) in such a way that "the church effectively fulfills her responsibility through such instruments" (Canon 822.3).

2. Responsibilities Regarding Written Works and the Use of the Media of Social Communication

In the context of their duty to watch over the deposit of faith and preserve it intact (cf. Canons 386 and 747.1) and to satisfy the faithful's right to guidance in the way of sound doctrine (cf. Canons 213 and 317), the bishops also have the right and duty to:

a) "Be vigilant lest harm be done to the faith or morals of the Christian faithful through writings or the use of the instruments of social communication" (Canon 823.1).

b) "Demand that writings to be published by the Christian faithful which touch upon faith or morals be submitted to their judgment" (Canon 823.1).

c) "Denounce writings which harm correct faith or good morals" (Canon 823. 1).

d) Apply, as the case requires, those administrative and

penal sanctions provided for in the church's law to those who by infringement of the canonical norms abuse their proper office, constitute a danger to ecclesiastical communion or do harm to the faith and morals of the faithful (cf. Canons 805; 810.1; 194.1.2; 1369; 1371.1; 1389).

3. The Obligation to Take Action with the Proper Means

The moral and juridical instruments provided for by the church are placed at the disposal of the bishops for the safeguarding of faith and morals. Only if the church's pastors were to fail in their obligations could they neglect these instruments when the good of souls calls for and recommends them. Bishops should maintain continual contact with the cultural and theological world of their respective dioceses. In this way, any difficulties arising may be quickly resolved through a fraternal dialogue which provides the interested parties with an opportunity to make the needed clarifications. In following the procedures of canon law, disciplinary measures would be the last means to be applied (cf. Canon 1341), although it should not be forgotten that for the sake of good order in the church the application of penalties proves necessary in certain cases (cf. Canon 1317).

4. Particular Responsibilities of Diocesan Bishops

With due respect for the competence of the Holy See (cf. apostolic constitution *Pastor Bonus*, 48, 50-52) and that of episcopal conferences and particular councils (cf. Canon 823.2), bishops, inasmuch as they are pastors and the ones primarily responsible for correct teaching about faith and morals (cf. Canons 386; 392; 753; and 756.2), should make timely if prudent exercise of their right and duty of vigilance within their own diocese and proper jurisdiction. In fulfilling his responsibility, the bishop will also call the matter, when necessary, to the attention of the episcopal conference or particular councils or to the Holy See itself through the competent dicastery (cf. Canon 823.2).

5. The Assistance of Doctrinal Commissions

1. Doctrinal commissions, whether on the diocesan or episcopal conference level, should be a great help to bishops. The work of such commissions should be followed and encouraged because of the invaluable aid which they can offer the bishops in the fulfillment of their teaching mission (cf. Congregation for the Doctrine of the Faith, letter addressed to presidents of all the episcopal conferences, November 23, 1990).

2. The collaboration of people and institutions, such as seminaries, universities and ecclesiastical faculties, should also be sought. When they have the required competence in their disciplines and are faithful to the church's teaching, these too can make a contribution to the bishops in the fulfillment of their duties.

6. Communion with the Holy See

Bishops should maintain contact with the dicasteries of the Roman Curia and in particular with the Congregation for the Doctrine of the Faith (cf. Canon 360; *Pastor Bonus*, 48-55). To the doctrinal congregation should be referred those questions exceeding the bishops' competence (cf. *Pastor Bonus*, 13) or which for any reason indicate the appropriateness of action by or consultation with the Holy See. The bishops should also convey to the congregation all that has doctrinal relevance to the question, whether this be seen in a positive or negative light, along with their suggestions as to possible courses of action.

II.

Approval or Permission for Various Kinds of Written Works

7. *The Requirement of Approval or Permission*

1. Either approval or permission is required by the code for certain kinds of publications.

a) In particular, prior approval is needed for the publication of books of the sacred Scriptures and translations of them into the vernacular languages (cf. Canon 825.1), for catechisms and other writings dealing with catechetical formation (cf. Canons 775.2; 827.1), for textbooks dealing with those disciplines that touch on faith or morals and on which instruction is based in elementary, middle and also higher schools (cf. Canon 827.2).

b) Prior permission is required, on the other hand, for the Christian faithful to prepare and publish translations of the sacred Scriptures in collaboration with separated brothers and sisters (cf. Canon 825.2), for prayer books intended for public or private use (cf. Canon 826.3), for new editions of collections of decrees or acts issued by ecclesiastical authority (cf. Canon 828), for what is written by clerics and members of religious institutes for newspapers, magazines or periodicals which are accustomed to attack openly the Catholic religion or good morals (cf. Canon 831.1), for the publication of writings by members of religious institutes which deal with questions of religion or morals (cf. Canon 832).

2. Ecclesiastical approval or permission presupposes that the censor or censors, if more than one is considered appropriate (cf. Canon 830), found nothing objectionable; it guarantees that the writing in question contains nothing contrary to the church's authentic magisterium on faith or morals; and it attests that all the pertinent prescriptions of canon law have been fulfilled. It is appropriate, then, that in the act of granting the approval or permission itself explicit reference be made to the relative canon.

8. Writings for Which It Is Appropriate that the Local Ordinary Give His Judgment

1. The code recommends that books which deal with matters of sacred Scripture, theology, canon law, church history or religious or moral disciplines be submitted to the judgment of the local ordinary even if they are not employed as textbooks for teaching; the same is true for writings in which something is found of special concern to religion or to good moral behavior (cf. Canon 827.3).

2. The diocesan bishop, by virtue of his right to guard faith and morals in their integrity, could, if there were particular specific reasons, even require by an individual precept (cf. Canon 49) that such writings be submitted to his judgment. In fact, Canon 823.1 accords bishops the right to "demand that writings to be published by the Christian faithful which touch upon faith or morals be submitted to their judgment." No limitation is placed on this right save one of a general order, so that "the integrity of the truths of the faith and morals be

preserved." Such a precept could be imposed with regard to particular cases involving either individual persons or categories of persons (clerics, members of religious institutes, Catholic publishing houses, etc.) or with regard to specific subject matters.

3. In cases like these, ecclesiastical permission also carries the sense of an official declaration guaranteeing that the writing in question contains nothing contrary to the integrity of faith and morals.

4. If a writing contained opinions or questions which are specialized or in the domain of a particular expertise, and when it could cause scandal or confusion only in certain places or among certain people and not elsewhere, permission might be granted under specific conditions which would affect the way it is to be published or the language, but which, in any case, would make it possible to avoid the dangers involved.

9. Extending Approval or Permission

The approval or permission to publish some work applies only to the original text; this cannot be extended to new editions or translations of the same work (cf. Canon 829). A simple reprinting of a work is not considered to be a new edition.

10. The Right to Approval or Permission

1. Ecclesiastical permission constitutes both a juridical and a moral guarantee for the authors, the publishers and the readers. Thus, whether permission is required or only recommended, when a person requests it he has a right to receive an answer from the competent authority.

2. The examination preceding the granting of permission calls for the greatest of care and seriousness with consideration given both to the rights of the authors (cf. Canon 218) and those of all the faithful (cf. Canons 213, 217).

3. When permission or approval is denied, administrative recourse in accordance with Canons 1732-1739 can be had to the Congregation for the Doctrine of the Faith, which is the dicastery competent for such questions (cf. *Pastor Bonus*, 48).

11. *The Competent Authority for Granting Approval or Permission*

1. According to the norm of Canon 824, the competent authority for granting approval or permission is either the proper local ordinary of the author or the ordinary of the place in which the work is to be published.

2. If permission is denied by one local ordinary, recourse may be had to the other competent ordinary. There is the obligation, nonetheless, to make the fact of the prior refusal of permission known. The second ordinary is not to grant permission without having learned from the first ordinary his reasons for denying it (cf. Canon 65.1).

12. *The Procedure to Be Followed*

1. Before giving permission, the ordinary should submit the writing in question to the judgment of people he holds as reliable. It may be that he chooses them from a list compiled by the episcopal conference or he may consult the commission of censors, if one has been established in accordance with the norm of Canon 830.1. In giving his judgment, the censor should follow the criteria given in Canon 830.2.

2. The censor should give his judgment in writing. If the judgment is favorable, the ordinary should give the permission in his own name, detailing the date and place it was granted. If he were to judge, however, that granting permission is not opportune, he should communicate the reasons for this to the author (cf. Canon 830.3).

3. Relations with authors should always be carried on in a constructive spirit of respectful dialogue and ecclesial communion so that ways may be found to ensure that nothing contrary to the church's doctrine comes to be published.

4. Information concerning the granting of permission should be printed in a place readily noted in the books which are published. Thus, it is not sufficient to use the formula "with ecclesiastical approval" or something similar; the name of the ordinary who gives his permission as well as the date and place in which it was given ought to appear in print (cf. the authentic interpretation of Canon 830.3: *Acta Apostolicae Sedis* 79, 1987, 1249).

13. Permission to Write for the Various Communications Media

The local ordinary should give careful consideration whether and in what circumstances permission might be granted to clerics or religious to write for newspapers, magazines or periodicals which are accustomed to attack openly the Catholic religion or good morals (cf. Canon 831.1).

III.

The Apostolate of the Christian Faithful in the Publishing Field, Particularly in Catholic Publishing Houses

14. The Commitment and Cooperation of All

The Christian faithful who are employed in the publishing trade, which here includes the sale and distribution of written works, have, in accordance with their specific tasks, a proper and particular responsibility for the promotion of sound doctrine and good morals. They are not only bound therefore to avoid cooperating in the distribution of works contrary to faith and morals, but they should make positive efforts toward the dissemination of written works which contribute to the human and Christian welfare of their readers (cf. Canon 822.2-3).

15. Publishing Houses Under the Sponsorship of Catholic Institutions

1. Publishing concerns sponsored by Catholic institutions (dioceses, religious institutes, Catholic associations, etc.) have a particular responsibility in this area. In consideration of the special link they have with ecclesiastical authority, their activities should be conducted in harmony with the church's doctrine, in communion with her bishops and in conformity with her laws. Catholic publishers are not to issue works which do

not have the prescribed ecclesiastical permission.

2. Publishing houses sponsored by Catholic institutions ought to be an object of particular concern for local ordinaries so that their publications always conform to church teaching and make an effective contribution to the good of souls.

3. Bishops have an obligation to prevent the sale and display in their churches of publications which deal with questions of religion or morals and have not received the permission or approval of church authority (cf. Canon 827.4).

IV.

The Responsibility
of Religious Superiors

16. General Principles

1. Religious superiors cannot be considered authentic teachers of the faith in a proper sense, and they are not, strictly speaking, pastors. They do, however, possess a power which comes from God through the ministry of the church (Canon 618).

2. Apostolic action on the part of religious institutes is to be exercised in the name and by the mandate of the church and should be carried out in communion with her (Canon 675.3). The prescription of Canon 209.1 on the obligation which all the Christian faithful have always to maintain communion with the church in their patterns of activity has particular application in the case of religious. Canon 590 gives a reminder to institutes of consecrated life regarding their special subjection to the supreme authority of the church and the bond of obedience which binds their individual members to the Roman pontiff.

3. Along with the local ordinary, religious superiors have the responsibility of granting permission for the publication of writings dealing with questions of religion or morals by members of their institutes (cf. Canons 824 and 832).

4. All superiors, especially those who are ordinaries (cf. Canon 134.1), are obliged to take care that within their institutes ecclesiastical discipline is followed also as regards the instruments of social communication. If abuses emerge, they are to insist upon its application.

5. Religious superiors, especially those whose institutes are dedicated precisely to the apostolate of the press and the social communications media, should see to it that their members faithfully follow the pertinent norms of canon law. They should give special attention to publishing houses, bookstores, etc., associated with the institute, to encourage their being faithful and effective vehicles for the church and her magisterium.

6. Religious superiors should cooperate with diocesan bishops (cf. Canon 678.3); it may be that such cooperation is even formalized through written agreements (cf. Canon 681.1-2).

17. Permission of the Religious Superior

1. The religious superior, who in accordance with Canon 832 is competent to grant his own religious members permission to publish writings dealing with questions of religion or morals, should not proceed to do so until he has the prior judgment of at least one censor he considers reliable and is satisfied that the work does not contain anything which might be harmful to the doctrine of the faith or morals.

2. The superior can require that his permission precede that of the local ordinary and that explicit mention of the fact be made in the publication.

3. This permission can be given in a general fashion when it is a question of an ongoing collaboration in the publication of periodical literature.

4. It is particularly important that in this area too there be good cooperation between local ordinaries and religious superiors (cf. Canon 678.3).

18. Religious Publishing Houses

What has been said in general about publishing houses sponsored by Catholic institutions is applicable in the case of publishing houses sponsored by religious institutes. Their publishing efforts should always be looked upon as apostolic works which are to be pursued by mandate of the church and carried out in communion with her, in fidelity to the proper charism of the institute and in obedience to the diocesan bishop (cf. Canon 678.1).

This instruction was adopted at an ordinary meeting of the Congregation for the Doctrine of the Faith and was approved at an audience granted to the undersigned cardinal prefect by the supreme pontiff, Pope John Paul II, who ordered its publication.

Given in Rome, at the Congregation for the Doctrine of the Faith, March 30, 1992.

Cardinal Joseph Ratzinger
prefect

Archbishop Alberto Bovone
secretary

St. Paul Book & Media Centers

ALASKA

750 West 5th Ave., Anchorage, AK 99501 907-272-8183.

CALIFORNIA

3908 Sepulveda Blvd., Culver City, CA 90230 310-397-8676.

1570 Fifth Ave. (at Cedar Street), San Diego, CA 92101 619-232-1442

46 Geary Street, San Francisco, CA 94108 415-781-5180.

FLORIDA

145 S.W. 107th Ave., Miami, FL 33174 305-559-6715; 305-559-6716.

HAWAII

1143 Bishop Street, Honolulu, HI 96813 808-521-2731.

ILLINOIS

172 North Michigan Ave., Chicago, IL 60601 312-346-4228; 312-346-3240.

LOUISIANA

4403 Veterans Memorial Blvd., Metairie, LA 70006 504-887-7631; 504-887-0113.

MASSACHUSETTS

50 St. Paul's Ave., Jamaica Plain, Boston, MA 02130 617-522-8911.

Rte. 1, 885 Providence Hwy., Dedham, MA 02026 617-326-5385.

MISSOURI

9804 Watson Rd., St. Louis, MO 63126 314-965-3512; 314-965-3571.

NEW JERSEY

561 U.S. Route 1, Wick Plaza, Edison, NJ 08817 908-572-1200.

NEW YORK

150 East 52nd Street, New York, NY 10022 212-754-1110.

78 Fort Place, Staten Island, NY 10301 718-447-5071; 718-447-5086.

OHIO

2105 Ontario Street (at Prospect Ave.), Cleveland, OH 44115 216-621-9427.

PENNSYLVANIA

214 W. DeKalb Pike, King of Prussia, PA 19406 215-337-1882; 215-337-2077.

SOUTH CAROLINA

243 King Street, Charleston, SC 29401 803-577-0175.

TEXAS

114 Main Plaza, San Antonio, TX 78205 512-224-8101.

VIRGINIA

1025 King Street, Alexandria, VA 22314 703-549-3806.

CANADA

3022 Dufferin Street, Toronto, Ontario, Canada M6B 3T5 416-781-9131.